Old Age Doesn't Have to Suck... Entirely

By Trish Sara

Rated MW for Mature Women
Includes Strong Language, Sex References and Violence
Alluded to

Published in 2024 by Trish Sara

Copyright © Trish Sara 2024

The moral rights of the author have been asserted.

All rights reserved. No part of this book may be reproduced or transmitted by any person or entity, including internet search engines or retailers (including but not restricted to, Google and Amazon), in any form or by any means, electronic or mechanical, including photocopying (except under the statutory exceptions provision of the *Australian Copyright Act 1968*), recording, scanning or by any information storage and retrieval system without the prior written permission of the author.

The author expressly prohibits any entity from using this publication in any manner for purposes of training artificial intelligence (AI) technologies to generate text, including without limitation technologies that are capable of generating works in the same style or genre as this publication. The author reserves all rights to licence uses of this work for generative AI training and development of machine learning language models

Cover and illustrations by Ben Wier.

CONTENTS

1. You're Only as Old as You Feel
2. Clothes Make the Woman
3. We Aren't as Smart as We Used to Be?
4. We Aren't as Attractive as We Used to Be?
5. We Aren't as Healthy as We Used to Be?
6. Ageism Sucks
7. Family, Friends and Their Role in Our Life
8. The Changes We Choose
9. The Changes We Don't Choose
10. The Story We Tell Ourselves
11. Bits and Pieces
12. Postscript

Foreword

I should tell you upfront, I'm no expert on ageing. However, over the past few years I've taken an interest in what inspires and depresses me about ageing.

To quote Bridget Jones, I've made "notes to self". In this book I share my observations and offer some of the conclusions I've come to in the hope these may be helpful in your ageing process. I've written for women in the main. Men, after all these years, are still somewhat of a mystery to me. I haven't gilded the lily, as my mum used to say. There are certainly some significant challenges in ageing; the loss of friends and family to illness, then death, the body's refusal to operate as it once did, the face you see in the mirror that doesn't reflect how you feel inside.

But old age doesn't have to suck entirely. Of that I am absolutely convinced.

So much of what we feel and focus on as we age are preconceived ideas about what it is to be old. They come from memories of our parents and their generation, stories, the media in all its forms, and even from comedians.

Two of my favourite Australian comedians are Judith Lucy and Denise Scott, both of whom have had long and successful careers. I've been to all their shows and, over the years, have enjoyed their hilarious takes on everything from dating to getting old. And while I've howled with laughter and shed tears of mirth about their experiences of aging, a part of me also feels sad that we take the piss about the negative aspects of ageing and ignore the amazing doors that open as we age.

You may be thinking, "Well, how old are you?" I'm 68. Not too far into old age, but old enough to know my journey of life is more than three quarters through (if I'm lucky) and time is too precious to waste.

Trish Sara.
BCouns (Coaching), DipCouns.

Chapter 1

You're Only as Old as You Feel

Bollocks!

I did a Google search to find out who coined the phrase, and while I found a host of articles on the topic, I could not find from whom this wisdom first came. I assume they've fallen off their mortal coil by now and aren't feeling anything at all.

Some days I feel a hundred years old when: I roll out of bed, aching with every movement, having slept badly on my dodgy shoulder, or when I vainly try to cut my toenails and can't quite reach my toes because I've become so inflexible.

Or when I've been playing bucking horse on the floor with my grandson and find I must get on all fours to raise myself to vertical with the aid of a nearby coffee table. In the meantime, he's leapt up and is halfway to his next adventure. Meanwhile, I'm texting my physio to check his next availability!

In fairness, I suspect the meaning of the phrase may not have been about how we feel physically, but how we feel within.

When a woman of around my age starts a sentence with "Of course at our age…" my first impulse is to stick myself in the eye with a fork, just to cut short her next words.

They are generally along the lines of:

- We aren't able to wear the clothes we used to
- We aren't as smart/sharp as we used to be
- We aren't as attractive as we used to be
- We aren't as healthy/fit as we used to be

We aren't, we aren't, we aren't, we aren't. Just stop it! And stop saying "we". Speak for yourself! Let me address each of these in turn.

Chapter 2

Clothes Make the Woman

If you've always found dressing 'on trend' a pain in the arse, old age is the perfect time to say, "To hell with it. I will wear track pants and comfy shoes."

Conversely, if you love fashion, you don't have to follow trends slavishly. You can pick and choose and invent your own style, one that makes you feel happy and self-expressed.

Some fashion trends I'm more than happy to leave behind, thank you very much.

G-Strings

I tried wearing a G-string some years ago while on holiday in Thailand with a girlfriend. My daughter had convinced me G-strings were comfortable undies with no panty line and they wouldn't take up much room in my bag. I'm a light traveller.

I realised my mistake when we went to an elephant reserve and took a trek through the jungle. It was deathly hot and humid. About half an hour into the experience, I felt the G-string relentlessly working its way into the flesh of my crack as the elephant swayed from side to side along the narrow pathway.

By the end of the trek, I had to be assisted from the elephant. Dying for a pee, I dashed to the closest loo, a squat style with footplates either side. Great!

My girlfriend stood outside while I removed the thong from between my raw buttocks, moaning with every movement. When finally extracted, it looked like a piece of dental floss! I went the remainder of the day sans undies.

Thong Swimwear (not the footwear)

See above and add sand.

High Heels

There are some things I wouldn't dream of wearing now, six-inch heels for starters. I'd need a walking frame to keep myself upright.

The last time I wore a decent pair of heels I walked like a trans person the morning after Gay Mardi Gras. And of course, we don't want to have 'a fall' at our age.

Ripped Jeans

While I like the ripped look, the ones with the knees totally ripped open have no appeal to me. They're cold in winter and these days my knees (which have always been knobbly) look like angry pug faces.

Tiny, tiny shorts, skirts, tops, etc

When I was a teenager in the 70s, mini skirts the size of an armband were in fashion. They were just long enough to cover the crotch of your knickers. Going up stairs or escalators was a tag team event, one girlfriend covering the butt of the other while ascending. The last girl up the stairs/escalators used her handbag to cover her own butt.

Getting out of a car without showing what your gynaecologist should only ever see was mission impossible, and if you dropped something on the footpath... well you just had to kick it the curb and cut your losses.

Toplessness and Bralessness

Some of my girlfriends now find it convenient to forget the braless and topless era of the 70s and 80s.

I didn't find going braless a challenge. Mine were so small they could barely fit a trainer bra. One of my friends, however, was blessed with magnificent breasts, each of which could fit neatly into a champagne glass (not the flute shape). However, she was self-conscious about her nipples being obvious and hated men ogling them.

Her solution was to wear band-aids over her nipples. Unfortunately, and for reasons I still don't understand, she chose square band-aids, giving her the appearance of having square areola, thus attracting more attention.

In the 80s, being topless on the beach in Sydney was more common than not. I was at Balmoral beach one day and watched a young man in a dark suit purposefully working his way up the beach with a bible tucked firmly under his arm.

He squatted down, uninvited, next to every topless woman he came across and proceeded to quote from the bible, presumably about the sins of the flesh.

He must have known chapter and verse by heart because his glassy little eyes never left their breasts.

I could see each woman mouthing expletives at the man who, unperturbed, happily continued his work for God along the beach. I imagine he was calling God's name that night as he caressed himself to sleep.

The topless era phased itself out within a few years, presumably because women got tired of men such as the God botherer I've just described.

Shapewear

Many years ago, I worked as a public relations consultant for a company whose office manager was a stout little woman with a tight bun and horn-rimmed glasses worn on a chain, which dangled over her copious bosom. Alma was a good old sort, but highly suspicious of young people.

I found her in the bathroom one day, bent over with laughter, a rare and alarming sight.

She explained that she had been convinced most of the staff were on cocaine. I was surprised she knew much about drugs and asked how she'd come to this conclusion.

Between gasps, she told me that she had found a trail of white powder in the corridors, leading into each of the consultant's offices.

Like a bloodhound she took a pinch of the suspect powder, smelled it and rubbed it between her fingers. She may even have rubbed a little on her teeth (as seen on TV cop shows). She went to our employer to report her suspicions.

It was only when she visited the loo later that she realised the powder was following her. On closer inspection she realised *her* corset was the cause.

It had perished over time and over extension, and was literally disintegrating every time her legs rubbed together, leaving a trail of white powder behind her.

Fast forward a few decades, and what used to be called corsets are reintroduced to women as 'shapewear', but with the same intended purpose: to cause as much discomfort as possible, pushing fat either inwards, upwards, downwards or wherever it could find its natural path.

When my daughter's wedding approached, I bought a lovely but figure-hugging dress to wear for the occasion. That was my first mistake. I then decided it was time to invest in some shapewear.

Come the big day, I needed the assistance of talc and my husband's foot firmly in the middle my back to squeeze myself into the shapewear.

Of course, once on, there was no possibility of going to the loo or eating more than a lettuce leaf all day. I walked as if in a body caste and couldn't bend at the waist.

And while it was one of the happiest days of my life, it was at the same time one of the most uncomfortable.

I wore the shapewear only once, then cut it into tiny pieces.

The wonderful thing about being a mature woman is that we have the choice to follow or not follow fashion trends. We can invent our own. Of course, we always had this choice, but I think you'll agree the pressure to be strictly on trend lessens with age.

I used to see an elderly woman in my suburb who wore the most exotic and colourful clothing. She used a walking frame but always wore high, glittery heels and brightly coloured exotic dresses.

After she died, a friend told me the woman had been a seamstress for the Tivoli Theatre and made most of the costumes for their extravagant shows, some of which she had kept. She made my day each time I saw her. I admired her confidence and disregard for what was expected of a woman of 'her age'.

In later life, my mother lived in an assisted living home in Ruschcutters Bay, just near Kings Cross. The home was full of colourful characters. It must have been a culture shock for a devoutly Christian woman such as Mum. One such character was a man who had decided, on the recent death of his wife, to live the remainder of his years as a woman.

He became Lorna. I often came across Lorna in the lift, invariably wearing a mauve cardigan, pink tulle skirt and matching converse with socks. There was nothing at all feminine about Lorna. She had a comb over, a prominent beer belly and a deep husky voice. But she carried herself with confidence and panache and no one ever challenged her life choice.

Old age provides us with the opportunity to be who we want to be, or whoever we've always wanted to be, and to hell with the opinion of others.

Over a cuppa with friends recently, I expressed this opinion regarding clothing, to which one friend replied, "…well of course, as long as what you wear is 'age appropriate'". I wondered how one was to establish what was 'age appropriate'. Is there a guide?

Chapter 3

We Aren't as Smart as We Used to Be?

I don't know that I'm qualified to write about this topic, but I'll give it a red hot go and it will be a short chapter.

One friend recently said "You're lucky, Trish. You've always been vague and forgetful, so you're probably not noticing any difference as you get older." I was stung by the comment, though had to agree it was true.

I have been known to ask a friend to hold on the phone when someone knocked at the door, only to totally forget I was on the phone at all, leaving her hanging and finally giving up.

I've forgotten about arrangements to meet a friend for lunch in the city, leaving her standing forlornly on a corner. One friend decided she would not meet me for lunch anymore, unless a third was invited. If I forgot to turn up, at least she could have lunch with someone.

I've forgotten that I relocated the iron to the clothes dryer to save storage space, then wondered why the dryer was making a loud clunking noise next time I used it.

I've taken my dog to an off-lead park and almost forgot to take him home. I've remembered to take my dog home but forgot to let him out of the car. Fortunately, I heard his whining, and it wasn't a hot day. I'm surprised my two children made it to adulthood.

The best example of my vagueness (is that a word?) dates to the 80s. As mentioned earlier, I was a public relations consultant for some years.

In the 80s, the accepted mantra was 'work hard, play hard'. I worked long hours and sometimes balanced this with boozy all-nighters.

One morning, I arrived home at 4am, which wasn't very smart as I had a presentation for a prospective new client the next day. I peeled off my leather pants and silk shirt, fell into bed and slept for a couple of hours before waking with a start. Shit, the presentation! Too late to consider what to wear, I pulled on the leather pants of the previous night and a clean shirt.

Surprisingly, even with a hangover, the presentation went very well indeed, and I won the account. Lunch was called for and I booked a swanky restaurant. The company was paying after all.

I strode through the restaurant feeling ten feet tall and very happy with myself; however, halfway to our table, I noticed a dragging sensation at my ankle. I looked down (at the exact time my new client did) to see one entire leg and half the crutch of the panty hose I had been wearing the previous evening dragging behind me on the carpet.

Stunned and embarrassed, I tried unsuccessfully to free the offending hose, which only made its grip tighter around my ankle. I had two options:

1. Walk to the Ladies Room with the panty hose still dragging behind, or
2. Grab the foot of the panty hose and hop/walk to the Ladies Room.

I chose the latter.

In future meetings, when presenting new campaigns to this client, I often wondered if he was thinking "Do I trust this woman with our account when she can't even dress herself?"

I have always been vague and, despite inventing ways to remind myself of things, I manage to forget them also.

My sisters, conversely, are whip smart and, despite being eight and ten years older than me, show no signs whatsoever of losing their marbles. They do Sudoku, the Cryptic Crossword and are long standing members of book clubs they have belonged to for decades. They read and discuss weighty books with their weighty brains.

I usually don't remember the name of the book or the author about ten minutes after I've turned the last page!

I challenge my brain by trying to remember where the hell I parked my car when I go to the shopping mall!

So, am I the best person to write on this topic? Probably not, but I do believe that we tend to put forgetfulness down to old age when it often isn't necessary. We are hyper alert and fearful of losing our mind. And while I acknowledge that some will experience dementia down the track, it serves no purpose whatsoever to look for signs on a daily basis.

Chapter 4

We Aren't as Attractive as We Used to Be?

My teenage daughter was going out bar-hopping one night with a girlfriend. The friend had arrived early and, while she was waiting, noticed a photo of my husband and I on our wedding day. She said, "Oh, you USED TO BE so pretty".

After taking several deep breaths to calm myself, I replied as was expected, with a polite "thank you, you're too kind". But in my imagination, I saw myself taking that bitch by her swan-like neck and squeezing it until her face turned the colour of an eggplant. Her doe-like eyes would bulge from her head like ping pong balls and eventually she would take her last breath. I'd drag her body into our garden, where I'd dig a deep hole and hear the satisfactory plop, plop of soil as I buried her.

Of course, it was a ridiculous fantasy. I wouldn't have time to do all that before my daughter appeared from the bathroom. Or would I?

My friends often talk about "losing their looks" as if they have simply misplaced them. Where have we lost them? Are they in that special place that everyone has in their home? The place where important things go, only to disappear forever?

But we haven't lost our looks. They've just changed and our faces are a reflection of the life we've lived and who we have been.

I realised this when attending a school reunion some years ago. I sat at a table with my old classmates and noticed their faces now reflected pretty much who they were and had always been.

There were five main types…

The Do-Gooders

These were by and large a decent (but boring) bunch. They generally belonged to ISCF (Inter School Christian Fellowship) and attended bible study each Wednesday in their lunch breaks. They never wore make-up, their hair was always squeaky clean and scraped back in a no-nonsense ponytail. Now, their faces told of a clean and moral life. They still wore no makeup, sensible shoes and comfortable clothes with elasticized waists.

The Disapprovers

These were the girls who had always worn their uniforms at the prescribed length (just below the knee) and their berets at the precise angle with no fringe showing. Their frown lines were now deeply etched in their disapproving faces, and their downturned mouths were a testimony to years of seeing the negative in everything and everyone.

The Dibby Dobbers

Similar in character to The Disapprovers, these girls were a whole other level. They had been prefects at school and policed the train station and playground with zeal. If high-viz vests had been around in our time, they would have worn these with PREFECT emblazoned on the back. They carried a pad and pen at all times to note and report any dissenters, and now their tight little pussy bum mouths told of many years judging others and finding them wanting.

The Popular Girls

We envied these girls with their pretty looks, confidence and boobs that seem to sprout overnight. They had real boyfriends (not the imaginary boyfriend of my fantasies) and hung out with them after school. Now they were a mixed bunch. Some had gone through several divorces and wore the bitter expression of disappointment. Others had invested in plastic surgery and other enhancements, and they had little expression, so it was difficult to imagine how their lives had fared.

Fringe Dwellers

I was lucky to find myself a great little group when I started high school. We couldn't be classified as Popular Girls. Perhaps Fringe Dwellers and Would-Be Popular Girls would be more accurate. We didn't obey the rules but managed to keep under the radar of The Disapprovers and Dibby Dobbers. We liked nothing more than taking the piss and discussing, fashion, makeup and what we knew or didn't know about the male species, particularly when it came to sex. How had our faces changed? I'd like to think we had aged well, crow's feet at the corner of our eyes and smile lines told of good times enjoyed. Though of course I could be biased.

The point I'm making here is that, while our faces may have aged, they tell a story about us and who we are.

Before I wrote this last paragraph, I had a good hard look at my face in the mirror, smiling then unsmiling.

Some people have faces that still look happy when not smiling. Mine isn't one of them. I look sad and a little stern. Is that what they call a Resting Bitch Face?

I have marionette lines from the corner of my mouth and lines on my forehead and sunspots that betray too many hours in the sun. But when I smile, I see a transformation that isn't too bad. The marionette lines diminish and, while the jowls don't entirely disappear, they reduce considerably. My eyes crinkle at the corners. They are eyes that have lived and laughed.

And without vanity, I think I can say I have a pleasant enough smile.

Don't laugh when I share this with you, but I had to practice smiling. I was a self-conscious girl, then a self-conscious woman. I cared too much about how I appeared and who was looking at me.

But I became acutely aware of the enormous benefits of having a good smile when taking my 99-year-old neighbour to a doctor's appointment in her wheelchair one day. As I pushed Fran along a busy footpath, I noticed that everyone walking towards us smiled broadly at her, whether they were young or old, male or female. Some even waved.

Fran had a wonderful smile. It was crooked, her teeth having worn more on one side than the other. But when Fran smiled, her face lit up with genuine warmth. And she greeted everyone we passed.

Later that day, I stood before the mirror and put on my usual smile to see what it looked like. Bloody Hell! It was more grimace than smile!

I never showed my teeth, the result of having braces for several years when a teen. In those days, braces weren't the near-invisible ones of today. They were heavy bands that made you look like Jaws from the James Bond movies.

I decided to change my smile. It took months of practice, but it was worth the effort. It felt stiff and forced at first, but now it's my natural smile.

As author, Stanley Gordon West once wrote "Smile and the world smiles with you."

Today, I'd like to think I have a good smile, a genuine smile when I pass strangers in the street. I often add a 'good morning' too and generally I receive the same in return. Why did it take me so long to learn this simple lesson?

And an added bonus is that it takes years off! No plastic surgeon, no injections! And you can move your face however you want. You can even raise an eyebrow.

The same can be said of your posture. Want to look younger, loose five kilos and appear several centimetres taller in an instant? Stand up straight, shoulders back. Be proud of your senior years and what you have achieved in your life.

I was going to write that as 'walk like a catwalk model', but scratch that. The way they stomp down the catwalk these days is scary. They look like they want to take to you with an axe. So don't do that. Please don't do that.

Chapter 5

We Aren't as Healthy as We Used to Be?

Have you seen the film *Flying High*? If not, you've missed one of the funniest movies of all time.

In one scene, the young, angst-ridden male star sits next to an elderly woman in a plane. She's sweet, polite and your classic 'old dear'. As soon as they buckle up, the young man starts on his life story. Her polite interest soon fades to a look of utter boredom, then desperation.

Ultimately, the poor dear hangs herself, having lost the will to live. You can see her feet dangling in the air while the young man continues to drone on about himself.

I've often felt this way when older people start on about their latest health issue. Arthritis, bunions, sleep apnea (them or their husband's, and that's a whole other conversation), osteoporosis, high/low blood pressure, varicose veins.

And it's not to diminish the pain my friends and I feel when we experience failing health. My husband

and I are responsible for keeping several pharmaceutical companies afloat!

But do we need to dedicate hours and hours to the topic of health?

Frankly, it's just plain boring to hear the minutiae of anyone's symptoms and medications, doctor and specialist visits, etc… Unless of course you're experiencing the same health issue, in which case any new information is devoured and discussed at length.

And, if you were honest with yourself, you'd agree… I think… Or am I a bad person?

While we're on the topic of health issues, would anyone have any tips or advice about how to treat UFO (Unexpected Fart Omissions)?

My mother suffered this affliction and sadly I've inherited the same.

Worse, Mum had both hearing loss and UFO, which meant she didn't know when she was letting one (or two, or three) rip.

Mum's dual afflictions first made themselves known in our home one day. She was walking across the living room farting loudly with each step. I stared daggers at my two young children for laughing. But let's face it, farts are funny. What else can you do?

I didn't laugh the first time I experienced a UFO. I was browsing in an upmarket boutique in a swanky Sydney suburb. It was the type of boutique staffed by gorgeous young things who give you the up and down when you enter, to establish whether you're worthy of or can afford their clothing.

A Michael Bublé song had just finished, and the next song hadn't started yet, when out it popped. It was a sharp, loud retort that couldn't be explained away as anything other than a fart.

It would have been far kinder had they laughed out loud and eased my embarrassment with a comment such as "don't worry it happens to all of us". But no.

Their eyebrows disappeared into their respective hairlines, eyes widened like fawns in headlights, and they swapped a glance that said, "We'll pretend we didn't hear it but can't wait until she leaves so, we can laugh ourselves sick."

Red in the face and fighting back tears, I pretended to consider several garments, then left. They couldn't even wait until I was out of earshot. Their laughter followed me to my car.

So, if you have any tips or advice on this matter, please contact me urgently, with the heading 'UFOs'.

In the meantime, I'll continue practicing my sphincter exercises rigorously.

Chapter 6

Ageism Sucks

Strap yourself in for this one. If you are offended by swearing, you might like to skip this chapter altogether because ageism really gets my goat. In fact, many 'isms' get my goat: sexism, racism, nepotism… athleticism.

I was visiting my mum at her retirement home one day when a staffer came to ask Mum if she wanted to join the art class. Mum was always short, but at 98 she was tiny, around four feet and ten inches in fact.

When the staffer came over to speak to mum, she squatted down, hands on knees, as if speaking to a toddler. In fairness, at Mum's height it was probably necessary. She tilted her head to one side, slapped on one of those smiles given to the simple minded and in a high voice (that people use for toddlers) asked her if she wanted to join the class.

I wanted to slap that condescending smile into tomorrow. I served the staffer with one of my best monologues.

It went something like this.

"My mother has lived through World War I, The Great Depression, World War II, the loss of her brother, and the imprisonment of her husband by the Japanese in Changi. During the war she did shift work in a munitions factory making bombs. She has lived for nearly 100 years and has more experience of life than you will probably ever have. Do not speak to her as if she is a child or an imbecile!"

I may have overreacted a little, okay a lot, and she was probably just being kind; but seriously why do we, in our culture, treat our older citizens like helpless simpletons?

And why do we change the language we use with older people?

I recently met up with my daughter at a large shopping complex. She was giving me instructions on the phone, about where her car was parked. I was on foot.

She asked what street I was in, so I was walking, talking and trying to read the street sign ahead.

The next thing I knew, I'd fallen off the gutter and into oncoming traffic. A nice bloke stopped his car to help me and another stopped the traffic.

I was okay, bar a few scratches and a bruised ego. I limped off to find my daughter.

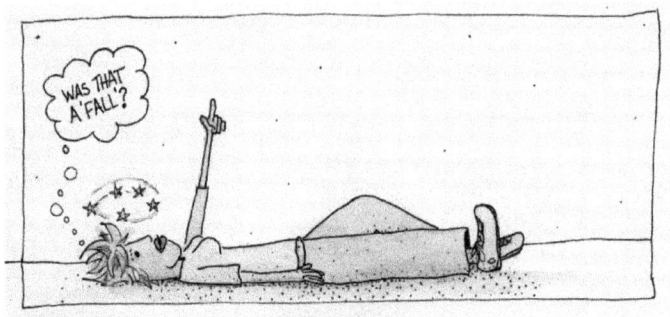

When I told the story, friends said, "Oh, you had a fall! Did you hurt your hip?" Because we all know when you break your hip that's the end of you. Before you know it, your family have whipped you into a nursing home and you're eating jelly for dessert for the rest of your life.

So why is it that when you're young, you simply fall over, but when you reach a certain age you've 'had a fall'?

When puzzling over this with a friend, she enlightened me. Apparently over the age of sixty you have a 'fall', and when you're 75+ it becomes a 'tumble'.

"Like a gymnast?" I asked.

She smiled sadly and took my elbow protectively as we crossed the road, presumably in case I had another fall.

In most non-Anglo cultures, older people are revered and respected for their wisdom. Not ours.

But I have to confess that I've been guilty of ageism myself. When I was young, our train station was right near a Senior Citizens Club. Once a week they had a Dance Afternoon. I'd hear the strains of Frank Sinatra, Eddie Nelson and Vera Lynn as I walked by. I saw old couples waltzing and, I'm ashamed to say, it always made me feel a bit depressed. I'm not sure why. Perhaps it was the thought of being old one day.

Just recently I was chatting with friends about how we used to love dancing. We bemoaned the fact that we were now too embarrassed to dance in public in fear of being ridiculed by younger people for our outdated moves.

I said, "Wouldn't it be great if we could hire a space, put on great music and just dance like we used to. We wouldn't allow young people, just guys our age." And then it occurred to me. What I was describing was exactly the same as the Senior Citizens Dance Afternoons.

On top of the shame I felt about this, I remembered how wonderful my parents had looked on the dance floor when they glided and dipped and danced cheek-to-cheek. It was, I reflected, so elegant, so sublime. I wish I could waltz.

We do need to work on changing others' perceptions.

Changing how others perceive older people is challenging of course. After all I've just described my feelings about Senior Citizens in my own past.

But, as the saying goes, you can't put old heads on young shoulders. Gees why would you want to? It would look creepy. And why would we want our young people to know what being older means? That's just mean. I don't want to know what it feels like to be 98!

My feeling is that we just have to get on with it and avoid the following:

Being a Biddy

You know who I'm talking about. The biddy in our street was Mrs Pitkin.

The venetians in her front room were permanently creased from her incessant peeking out to see what everyone was doing. She often reported to my mother about one of my sisters meeting up with various boyfriends on our corner to 'pash'.

She dobbed me in for taking off my school beret every morning when I got just around the corner and away from Mum's view... but not hers.

I don't think the woman slept, because it didn't seem to matter what time I got home, she had it noted, logged and reported to mother within 24 hours. These people are biddies because they don't have a life. So, if you're a biddy, my best advice is to get life for Christ's sake.

It seems every street has its biddy. I know who it is in our street. It's my husband.

He'll often comment that a certain neighbour must be on holidays because he hasn't seen their car for a week or so. He will offer the opinion that another neighbour must be selling soon, because he's seen men in smart suits and expensive cars entering their home and they've been doing a lot of painting and decorating lately.

But when I confront him about this issue and suggest he's the biddy in our street, he's affronted. According to him, only women are biddies, men are merely observant!

Starting sentences with "In our day..."

It seems some older people have a way of re-inventing history to suit the image they'd like to have of themselves in the past. And woe betide anyone who challenges them on their rose-coloured memories. We forget we were just as self-absorbed and reckless as anyone.

We conveniently forget all the dumb things we did.

You know when you're doing it. So, stop it!

Or I'll dob you into your children!

Complaining about today's generation

Older folk putting younger people down seems to be a reoccurring theme in history. As far back as the 1300s in fact.

"Modern fashions seem to keep on growing more and more debased... The ordinary spoken language has also steadily coarsened. People used to say 'raise the carriage shafts' or 'trim the lamp wick,' but people today say 'raise it' or 'trim it.'

- Tsurezuregusa (*Essay on Idleness*),
Yoshida Kenko 1300-1332

So, knowing that older people putting down younger people has been repeated over centuries, why do we still persist in doing it?

How can we say this generation is worse when we no longer put our children down mine shafts? When we are healthier and live longer than we ever have thanks to our young scientists and doctors? Our sons are the best fathers in history, sharing the load of childrearing. I could go on and on. This generation is doing a great job.

You will win no friends or respect by putting them down. You just sound bitter and jealous of their youth.

Telling younger people what they don't know

I remember having a heated exchange with my father when I was around 15. I wasn't allowed to go to the school dance, and I was distraught. Everyone else was going. We'd all talked about nothing else for weeks, had planned what we were going to wear, who we fancied, who we hoped to 'get with'.

In a fit of exasperation, Dad blurted, "You'll understand when you're a parent."

OMG I hated him right then.

It's a dirty card to deal, when people older than you say you'll understand when you're older, because they know you don't yet know. And you know they know you don't yet know. And you can't argue that. And as a young person, you just want to spit.

Before my firstborn arrived, older women who already had children couldn't wait to give me the benefit of their experience.

"You'll never have sex again, have a good night's sleep, have time for yourself."

Near the time of her birth, they couldn't wait to tell me about their 36-hour labour, the epidural that nearly left them permanently paralysed, and then there was this story…

Her husband and her only made it to the front drive of the hospital when the baby decided to arrive. She gave birth in the car at the entrance to the hospital.

When they wheeled her in, she told a nurse how embarrassed she was about giving birth in public.

The nurse told her it was nothing compared to the poor woman who had given birth near the reception desk in the middle of visiting hours several years earlier.

The nurse was fulsome in her description of the event. Apparently, children were screaming, people stood and gawped in horror and everyone got a very clear view of the event.

With a sigh, my friend said to the nurse, "Yes, I know. That was me too."

Following the birth of my own daughter, the advice never stopped. "You'll know you're alive when she starts crawling."

"You'll know you're alive when she starts walking."

It sucks to tell people uninvited what they don't yet know.

If you're tempted, I suggest you zip it

Chapter 7

Family and Friends and Their Role in Our Life

Family is everything?

Novelist Mary Karr once wrote that a dysfunctional family is any family with more than one person in it.

A friend recently commented that she knew the perfect family. The husband and wife adored one another. They were successful and attractive, she said, and their children had grown into lovely, well-adjusted and similarly successful adults.

I asked how often she met up with this family, to which she replied, "Oh once or twice a year."

My comment was, "Then you don't see them often enough to know."

If this sounds cynical, my bad. But I've found this to be true over time. There is no perfect family. We all have faults and failings; therefore so do our children, as will their children, and their children's children, etc. Infinitum.

I completed a bachelor's degree in counselling in my early 60s. In the final year, I did my practicum at an adult counselling service. I met with so many amazing and brave women who came from terrible circumstances: incest, domestic violence, both mental and physical.

How do these people feel when someone says, "family is everything". Pretty awful, I'm thinking. The reality is that families can keep you stuck and, at worst, destroy you.

Our birth families provide us with legacies, some good and some bad. And from an early age we work out where we have been placed in the family system. We are often given a label: the good child, the sensible child, the hard-working child, the naughty child, the intelligent child, the funny child.

Did you have a label in your family? These labels tend to stay set in families, and upsetting the status quo can be painful for everyone.

Okay, you may be thinking. This is a serious turn of events. What is she getting at?

I'll tell you…

It's timely, at this stage in our lives (if we haven't done so earlier) to review our place in the family and, if necessary, make changes to improve or even change our position. Hopefully we now have the maturity, wisdom and faith in ourselves to do so.

Say, for example, you've been the responsible one in your family. You're the one who always does what is expected. You're the one who organising a nursing home for your aged parent/s, the necessary paperwork, the management of their accounts, etc. You may be happy in this role and gain satisfaction from being the responsible one. That's great.

But maybe you're also tired of this role and didn't really ask for it in the first place.

Maybe you'd like to take a few months off to live in India and learn meditation, take up belly dancing, boot skootin' or have a shot at being a stand-up comedian.

Do you think any of this is going to be good news to your family? You bet your nellie it's not. Who's going to do all the stuff you've always done? Who will organise the sale of Mum and Dad's house when they die, who will arrange the funeral, cancel their banks accounts?

A shit storm is about to come your way because it means that everyone must be prepared to:

a. Accept and respect your choice
b. Make adjustments in the family system

But standing your ground on this issue is worth the pain, because now more than ever you know that life is short.

Change is difficult. Most of us hate change (a topic further on in this book). And if you change, it may mean that you're in the bad books for a while, or even excommunicated. You may be accused of being selfish.

You're not.

It may take months or even years to change your status within the family; however, it's a worthwhile endeavour to be the authentic, self-expressed person you want to be and not the child you once were.

If your family won't accept who you want to be, perhaps they need to look within to see why they feel this way. Hopefully it's something you can discuss as mature adults and not the kids you used to be.

And another BTW, your children may also have you stuck in a role you've grew out of long ago. They may not welcome the news that you're selling the family home to live a nomadic life while spending their inheritance. Get ready for that shit storm!

I recently watched a video joke. It was an older couple saying they had decided they didn't want children. Short pause…. "We're going to tell them tonight." Bahahaha!

Friends are The Family We Choose

True.

I generally don't like little plaques and cards with fluffy sayings hanging up on walls and in frames.

But a friend gave me a print with the above quote a few years ago and I love it, because it's true. Friends are the family we choose.

And one thing we sometimes take for granted as we get older, is the span of years we've enjoyed good friendships. The young are yet to enjoy this. It's a definite bonus of being older and one we sometimes forget to appreciate.

I'm lucky to have some amazing friends, who I've known since I was sixteen. That's over fifty years!

They've seen me through:

The pimply stage – I can't possibly come out tonight because I'm so ugly and no one will ever be attracted to me.

The Fat Stage – I can't go to the beach because I look like a beached whale. (I weighed 48 kilos when I said this!)

The Unrequited Love Stage – I can't go on without him. My life is over. (Actually, I've forgotten his name now!)

The Successful Career Woman Stage – I don't need a partner. I have a career. (Despite the fact that I cried myself to sleep at night wondering if I'd ever find love!)

I won't bore you with all the other stages I've been through and how tolerant and supporting my friends were through all my dramas.

Inevitably, some friends fall away with time. Their life goes on a different path, they move away or we just simply lose the connection we've had with them.

And sometimes, not often, a friend audit may be necessary.

Perhaps now is the time to do one?

Sometimes there are friends who we think should be life-long friends, because we've invested so many years in the friendship. But are they still bringing something to your life? When we meet with them, do we come away feeling uplifted, good about ourselves, supported? Or do we come away feeling drained?

Here's a checklist to help.

Does your friend:

Compete with you. Their children/grandchildren and husband are so amazing and doing so well, you feel that you've been dealt a dud hand. You haven't. Your friend lies through her teeth.

Good friends will share the good, the bad and the ugly. They'll tell you how pissed off they are with their kids/husband/brother/sister and won't hold back.

I meet with two friends most Fridays. Some people observe the Sabbath, we observe the Frideth. We meet for a meal and share everything, and I mean everything, from the state of our bodily functions to the children who refuse to leave home.

Steal your oxygen. Every conversation eventually leads back to them, just like all roads lead to Rome. For example, you've just arrived back from a holiday in Italy and all they want to do is tell you all about their holiday in Italy twenty years ago.

But when THEY go on a holiday, they'll make you sit through a two-hour video taken on a camera they stuck on their bike helmet.

Or worse, they'll make you sit in front of their computer while they show you 2,000 photos... and they insist on having control of the mouse so you can't just flick through at will!

In one case, a friend of mine not only gave a full and detailed description of the story behind every photo, but also what was over the hill from that photo!

Assume they know you better than anyone. They use your long friendship to imply they know you better than you do. "You've always been a drama queen/serious/negative" and so it goes on. These friends keep you stuck in a label and they want it to stay that way.

I'm not suggesting you should cut these friends off like a gangrenous limb, but it may be worth considering spending less time with them.

And if your friend ticks all three of the above checklist items, perhaps it's time to call in the surgeon!

Reconnecting with Old Friends

Now that we (hopefully) have a little more time and space in our lives, it may be worthwhile reconnecting with friends with whom you've lost contact.

I had a friend for whom I was a bridesmaid. She married young and moved to a suburb on the other side of Sydney. She had her children young. Whereas I married at 32 and had my children later.

A few years ago, we reconnected via Facebook and met up. And just like that, the decades melted away like ice cream on a hot pavement. We laughed so hard we nearly peed and haven't stopped since (laughing, not peeing).

Last year, she and another friend (her other bridesmaid) and I went to Vietnam for a holiday. We had a ball and will travel again together.

She calls my friend and I 'the bridesmaids'. We call her 'the bride'. She speaks with rounded vowels, dresses immaculately, and gives every appearance of being a lady. But what comes out of that potty mouth has us in stitches!

It was her birthday when we were in Vietnam so my other friend and I organised a birthday cake to be delivered to our table at the restaurant we'd booked for dinner.

What we didn't ask for was a singer to come to our table to sing *Happy Birthday,* with other guests invited to join in the song.

Happy Birthday sung in a high-pitched Vietnamese accent sounds like an out of tune violin. All eyes were turned to our friend. We videoed it. She smiled graciously, nodding her thanks (like a royal personage) to all and sundry while muttering out the side of her perfectly lipsticked mouth, "I'm going to effing kill you two when we get out of here".

I've looked at that video so many times. Still cracks me up.

Making New Friends

I urge you to consider the idea of making new friends.

I made a new friend a couple of years ago when I worked part-time in a new upmarket furniture showroom. I'll call her Lydia (because she still works there and could be fired if the boss reads this). Lydia is 45, which makes me 23 years older.

We quickly established a shared sense of take-the-piss humour. On quiet days, we could go several hours without a single customer. When a customer finally appeared, we'd murmur to each other "what the hell does sheeeeee want" before slapping on our best welcoming smiles.

After I left the company, we kept in contact. One day Lydia was having a particularly trying day at work with late deliveries and complaining customers, so I delivered her a Margarita disguised in a coffee sippy cup. She was most appreciative.

We talk often, meet for coffee or to shop, and our respective husbands get on like a house on fire. We were privileged to attend her wedding last year. She is a beautiful, big-hearted woman and I value our friendship. It feels as if there is no age gap.

She told me recently that she's always been attracted to old people. Ouch. But fair enough.

Some women feel their life is full enough keeping up with the children, grandchildren and their long-term friends; but here are some of the benefits of new friendships…

They don't know your life story. This means you can tell them all the stories that your friends have heard a million times and you don't have to worry about repeating yourself or boring them to death.

They keep you young. Some of my newer friends are at least ten years younger or more. I feel alive when I'm with them.

They don't know what you used to look like. Sometimes, when I meet with old friends I haven't seen for a while I wonder if they're thinking "Geez, she's let herself go." New friends don't know what you looked like without wrinkles and the spare tyre you've acquired with menopause. They know you just as you are.

They bring a new perspective to life.

They can even challenge you to do things you hadn't considered before, such as writing a book about old age.

Chapter 8

The Changes We Choose

Most of us don't like change. It can be uncomfortable and scary, and sometimes we become inflexible as we grow older, believing we can't or don't want change.

However, our ability to seek change, to keep learning about ourselves and the world around us, is without doubt a key to enjoying our senior years.

Author, artist and photographer Doe Zantama has this to say about resisting change.

"Every decision brings with it some good, some bad, some lessons, and some luck. The only thing that's for sure is that indecision steals many years from many people who wind up wishing they'd just had the courage to leap."

Embracing change can be the most liberating thing we do for ourselves as we age.

It is well documented and accepted that the brain is capable of setting down new neurological pathways throughout our life. This means we can adopt new ways of thinking with practice and intent. In short, we can continue to develop and grow as individuals.

Change can involve re-evaluating our values and taking a closer look at our strengths and how we can use, and building on these.

A Values Audit

In the final year of my counselling degree, I was at a class in which values were discussed. We were asked to do an exercise that the lecturer assured us would help establish our own values.

We were to spend half an hour writing our own obituary. The younger members of the class took to the exercise with relish. After all, they probably had years at their disposal to achieve who they thought they wanted to be and what they wished they would be remembered for.

I, on the other hand, felt a little freaked out by the task. I could see other older members in the class had the same reaction. One man, who would later finish his degree at the age of 80 (with a standing ovation at his graduation ceremony) looked particularly uneasy.

But in many ways, this exercise was a wake-up call and a life changer, not just for me but others in the class I suspect.

What did I hope friends and family would say about me when they gathered at my last hurrah? Would the attendees (which I hoped would be many) be smiling with fondness and nodding their heads in agreement? Would they chuckle at and sigh with admiration at stories of my humour, bravery and challenges met? Would they dab their tears away with moist handkerchiefs. Am I getting a little carried away?

Or would they be struggling over pen and paper, searching for something truthful but nice to say? Would my nearest and dearest have to make up something to gild the lily, as Mum used to say?

Has all this talk of obituaries got you down?

Read on for a light relief funeral story!

Fran's Funeral

I've spoken in an earlier chapter of my old friend Fran (the one who taught me to smile) who died at 101. She had married in her forties following World War II and had no children.

Her only living relatives were a niece and nephew, with whom she had nothing in common. She saw them rarely.

However, both were to benefit from her will, which left a very tidy sum to each.

According to Fran, the niece had always had her hand out. The niece was getting on in years herself and often wanted to benefit from Fran's money before she herself was too old to enjoy it.

For example, the niece once asked Fran to pay for singing lessons. The niece had convinced herself that she had the potential to develop her, as yet undiscovered, talent as an opera singer.

So, come the day of Fran's funeral, we gathered at the chapel of the nursing home. It was only a small group. When you live to a great age, your contemporaries have long passed and there are but a few left to bid you farewell. The congregation was sparse, comprising of the niece, the nephew, their children, a lady at the back row, whom I suspect attended each funeral as her weekly outing, the minister, pall bearers, my husband, two children and self.

As the ceremony came to a close, the minister called on Fran's niece to sing the last hymn.

She rose slowly from her pew with all the drama of a diva and walked to her stage. With one hand at her voluminous breast, handkerchief clutched in one hand, she let forth with the most appalling singing I have ever heard.

Having been raised in a devout Christian home, I thought some of the words in the hymn seemed familiar, but I could not for the life of me identify which hymn she was singing. Not one single note was in tune.

As the hymn continued, Fran's niece found her stride and confidence. Her throat and chins warbled alarmingly. Her hand shot out and upwards as if beseeching, her eyes closed then opened slowly as if to the heavens.

It was all too much for my family. Our pew started shaking, first from my daughter struggling with the effort not to laugh, then from the strain of our joint, unexpressed laughter. Fortunately, our family were the only ones sitting in the pew, but none of us dared to look at her or at each other.

I stared at Fran's coffin, half expecting her to raise the lid and shout, "well the singing lessons were a bloody waste of good money."

I miss my friend Fran, but the story of her funeral continues to be a family favourite.

Back to my classroom exercise in values. At the end of the half-hour to write our own obituaries, we were asked to review what we had written, and ask what values we could identify as most important to us.

For example, some listed that they would like to be remembered for their generosity, truthfulness, honour, altruism, valuing family above all, being open minded, true to their friends, a good mother, and so on.

The idea, of course, was to gauge how were we faring with each of these to date. What importance did we give to these values in our day-to-day lives?

The next step of the exercise was then to draw a circle, and divide the circle (like pie pieces) by labelling each piece with the values we had identified.

Next, we were to fill in each pie piece indicating the percentage effort we were currently giving each of our values.

While I liked to think my values were in balance, I had to admit that way too much of my time and effort was focussed on some values, while others languished.

The exercise gave me the opportunity to stand back from my life and take stock of what was really important to me. If you have half an hour or so to spare, I'd highly recommend this exercise.

The Strengths Test

While studying my degree, my favourite unit by far was Positive Psychology. And my all-time favourite author on the subject is Martin Seligman PhD, widely acknowledged as the father of Positive Psychology. He's written many books on the subject, including *Flourish*, which I'd highly recommend.

Together with Christopher Peterson PhD, the two developed the VIA Character Strengths Test, which I'd recommend as a great place to start if you'd like to identify and grow your strengths. The test is free and will only take about 15 minutes to complete through a questionnaire process, which will identify your strengths, listed from 1 to 25. You can find it by searching 'VIA Strengths Test'.

Don't pay too much attention to the lower ranking strengths, rather focus on your top five.

I was surprised at the results of my own test, but really resonated with each of my five strongest. This gave me the impetus to think about how I could use my greatest strengths to improve my satisfaction in life, and therefore thrive.

When we reported on our strengths in the next Positive Psychology class, most students identified impressive strengths such as Altruism, Compassion, and Honesty. All very honourable strengths for would-be counsellors.

My top two were 'Humour' and 'A love and Appreciation of Beauty'. I felt a bit embarrassed. Surely these strengths were not important for someone wanting to be a counsellor?

However, when I read a description of these strengths, I realised they were both useful and important.

Being aware of the beauty in nature and art helps in mindfulness practice, taking the mind away from dark thoughts and focussing on the beauty around us.

Similarly, a sense of humour can, in some circumstances, lighten a heavy atmosphere and bring some relief, if only momentarily.

By this, I don't mean I ever made a joke of counselling my client's circumstances; but I did often find it helpful to use a little self-deprecating humour to remind clients that I didn't know everything, and sometimes I was a fool and made mistakes.

There are a host of exercises to help in developing our better selves, and you don't need to be a therapist to understand them.

Chapter 9

The Changes We Don't Choose

A Pity Party for One – A Personal Perspective

The year 2017 was one of the happiest of my life. My daughter gave birth to our first grandchild, my son met the love of his life (who would later become his wife), and I finally finished my degree in Counselling and Coaching.

To understand how proud I felt, my three older sisters had all been awarded scholarships to Sydney University when they completed their Higher School Certificates. Whereas I had left school at 15 and, while I had forged a successful career, I had never quite felt their equal.

When I walked up the steps to the podium to receive my degree, wearing mortar board and gown, I felt unexpectedly taller and proud of myself. I walked on air.

That same year, my husband and I decided to downsize and put a deposit on an off-the-plan apartment on the Northern Beaches of Sydney. Having grown up in Sydney's Western Suburbs, where the closest beach was a long hot drive away, it was a dream come true.

I planned to buy a kayak and paddle the lagoon near our apartment, enquired about joining a local dragon boat team and doing a sculpture course, and I bought a bike to cycle around our new suburb. I had so many plans for my retirement!

A regular mammogram changed it all. When asked to come in for further tests, I was concerned but not overly.

When asked to attend a further meeting with an oncologist and a counsellor, my heart sank. Counsellors don't attend meetings to share good news. The obligatory tissue box sat on the table with a glass of water.

Five years later, and the cancer has not returned. However, I now have severe nerve damage in one hand and this has changed my life.

My dreams of riding a bike, kayaking, learning to sculpt and dragon boat racing have had to be shelved. I can only type one-handed, which is slow and frustrating for someone who loves to write.

In fact, I stopped writing this book for two years. During this time, I couldn't write about old age not entirely sucking because, deep down, I don't think I believed it to be true, as much as I professed otherwise.

All the wonderful learning I'd gained through counselling seemed to fade into the background. I didn't use any of the Positive Psychology practices I had previously found so helpful for me and my clients. I had a Pity Party and invited no one but myself.

My dad used to say that if you lost a leg, it isn't always possible to look at a person who had lost two legs and be grateful.

I tried to practice my daily routine of listing three things I was grateful for, and other positive therapy exercises, but I was just going through the motions.

I slept a lot. I gave up exercise altogether and often let phone calls go to voicemail.

I wish I could tell you how I brought myself out of that stage. There was no pivotal event. But I think a turning point came when my family kept asking me if I was okay.

I hated the thought of being seen as sad and pathetic.

So, for the first time, I shared my thoughts and feelings with those who were very close me, and this brought about a shift. I didn't feel as alone. The Pity

Party stopped. Not due to any force of will, it was just time to get on.

Many people reading this chapter will have experienced far greater challenges than me. I don't write about my own experience to garner sympathy. Not at all.

The point is that, as we grow older, we are more likely to experience changes that are extremely difficult, and there is no shame in taking however long it takes to accept the unwanted changes that come our way.

But, it can help to reach out to others, whether they be close friends, family or professional therapists.

Anyway, enough of the dreary stuff. We know that living in the past, and mulling over it, is a waste of time; and fretting about the future is pointless. At this stage in our lives (and at any stage), life can change in a heartbeat.

But living in the moment and squeezing the juice out of life is a skill, and now is a good time to learn it and hone it.

Here are some practices that have and haven't worked for me, which may or may not work for you.

Swimming

For me, swimming works. It combines exercise (no jarring joints hitting the pavement) and mindful meditation. With nothing to distract me other than the line at the bottom of the pool, I find I can go into a trance-like meditative state. The only drawbacks are:

1. People who aren't aware that their cozzies when wet and past their use-by-date, such that they are almost totally transparent. Erk!
2. The occasional discovery of small, pebble-like poos resting on the bottom of the pool. If you don't believe me, ask any pool attendant and

they will tell you that scooping pellets out with a net on a pole is part of their job spec.

Now I've moved to the beach, I have access to an ocean pool, where thankfully the only pebbles I see are of the seaside variety. I swim most days in summer. Yesterday I walked down to the pool in the late afternoon and found myself bobbing and floating about with several people, about my own age, with this big ocean pool all to ourselves. Bliss.

I reflected on what a contrast it was to be swimming laps when I was a young executive. I used to rise at 6am and swim three kilometres most weekdays, along with other workers, briefcase stowed in a locker while I focussed on the day ahead, stroking out my anxiety with every lap. The pool was invariably crowded. There was the odd kick in your face or a shoulder charge if you weren't keeping pace.

What a different experience it was now. Yep, I hate the way my legs look all wobbly because the skin has lost its zing and the varicose veins are like rope... all of that.

But you don't get to have it all at any time in your life, and I feel that what I have now is a pretty good trade.

Walking

I've never been much of a runner/jogger, my style being similar to Cliffy Young, the potato farmer famous for winning the Sydney to Melbourne Ultra Marathon at the age of 61. His style was called the Cliffy Young Shuffle. My jogging style is more a Trish Has Had a Stroke Shuffle!

These days, I enjoy long walks with a friend each week around Narrabeen Lagoon. The walk is about 12 kilometres, with thoughtfully planned public toilets at intervals for the weaker of bladder. My friend and I have ranked each toilet block for cleanliness, toilet paper quality and quantity and privacy.

I used to take my dog with us. On one of our walks, he felt the need to check if I was okay in the toilet. He pushed the door, which couldn't be locked, with his snout, exposing me to a group of joggers.

He doesn't come with us anymore.

Yoga and Pilates

An amazing practice for the mind and body, but not for me. Refer to Chapter 5 regarding UFOs (Unexpected Fart Omissions). Could there be anything more mortifying than doing a Down Dog when the room is completely quiet, bar the soft expulsion of breath and the sound of one's buttocks letting one down.

Years ago, I also tried hot yoga. Being post-menopausal, my internal thermostat is dicky at the best of times. In a room of heaving sweaty bodies, with my nose a metre from the groin of a man with legs spreadeagle (revealing one shrivelled testicle peaking from his not-tight-enough undies), I found myself crawling for the door on all fours. Once outside the room, I wretched uncontrollably for a moment before escaping outdoors where I took great gasping breaths of blessedly fresh air.

Meditation

I've tried over and over to meditate, and it is, I'm assured, the most amazing thing you can do for your wellbeing, particularly as it relates to living in the moment.

I've tried meditating in bed (couldn't get comfortable, then drifted off to sleep), while sitting on a beach (sand in my pants), in a group setting (couldn't resist peeking and checking out neighbouring meditators and thinking about what colour I wanted to paint my walls), all to no avail.

There is a host of free apps to help with meditating. My son meditates on the hour-long bus ride to work each morning. It's something you can do virtually anywhere and anytime.

Being Creative

I used to get together with two other friends once a month for a painting date. We'd take turns hosting lunch, then settle into an afternoon of painting and chatting.

I'd become very frustrated, however, that I never managed to produce anything I'd be happy to hang on a wall.

Our painting days went on hold for a couple of years; however, we've recently resumed, and I love our days together. I've changed my attitude to painting and have decided that the joy of being creative is enough. My art doesn't have to be gallery worthy.

An adjustment of attitude can change so much of your pleasure in life.

Writing also gives me great pleasure. You know when you're doing something mindful, because time flies.

What gets your own creative juices flowing? When does time fly for you?

Altruism (giving without needing anything in return)

The act of giving can be enormously gratifying and uplifting. It doesn't have to be grandiose or involve a lot of time or money. In fact, some acts of altruism are very simple and can be practiced without effort every day.

Here are some simple things that improve my mood every single day:

- Smiling at passers-by with a heartfelt "Good Morning" or "Hi".

- Complimenting someone... on their lovely smile, a colour they're wearing, an outfit, on anything at all. It puts a spring in the step of the recipient, and it feels good to have done so. Older women, like ourselves, particularly appreciate a compliment. We don't receive them often enough and a well-placed, sincere compliment can make someone's day.

- For older men, a compliment invariably met with a wide grin means "You'll go far young man!" and they love it.

- Thanking the people who serve us daily and commenting on how well they do their job. It's sad to see signs everywhere these days asking people not to abuse serving staff. When did this become necessary!

It's not difficult or time-consuming to do any of these acts and the cumulative effect in a day is highly rewarding. We all crave being acknowledged and appreciated.

Chapter 10

The Story We Tell Ourselves

It's said that what happens in our lives is not as important as the way we view our story.

I've known people who have had awful things happen to them, events they did not deserve and in which they had no control. And yet these people manage to view their story as being a path to who they are. They choose to see the positive. They are content.

Conversely, I know a man who came from great wealth and privilege, yet continually sees himself as a victim. He doesn't work; he doesn't need to and in fact hasn't for many years. He lives in a multi-million-dollar home in a fashionable suburb. Still, he blames his background and being indulged for his constant dissatisfaction with life.

Changing our story isn't easy. In class one day, we were asked to write a brief story about something bad that had happened in our life. Something that had had a negative impact on us and the way we saw ourselves.

Task completed, we were then asked to read our story to each individual in the class (about 15 people) one by one, sitting in front of each person.

About twenty minutes into the exercise, reading our stories aloud, over and over, the teacher asked, "are you sick of it yet?"

Most of the stories were hard to hear and sad. And yet, surprisingly, we all sighed then laughed. We were indeed sick of our story and after many repetitions it seemed futile to repeat it yet again.

Don't get me wrong. It's important to know our story in terms of helping us to understand our behaviours and why we feel the way we do and react to certain things.

I'll give you a personal example. One of my sisters was a bully and loved to tease me when I was little. She'd sometimes invite me to step into the broom cupboard (I was very gullible), then slam the door shut behind me.

She'd tell me I had ten minutes of air before suffocating. She'd count off the minutes and periodically ask if it was getting harder to breathe. When ten minutes was about to expire (in reality it was probably more like two or three minutes), she'd fling open the door. I'd fall out onto the linoleum floor, at her feet, gasping for breath.

We were never close. I haven't seen or spoken to her for decades.

This sister had, and probably still has, a large, wide mouth. Consequently, and quite unconsciously, I never liked women with big, wide mouths. Until I understood the connection. Crazy, I know. But because I now understand this about myself, I can enjoy a Julia Roberts movie without wanting to slap that big, beautiful smile off her face.

There is a world of difference between self-exploration to understand our life, and how it has impacted the way we are, and getting stuck in our story.

The past does not have to predict our future

I recently met a man to do an interview for our local media. He owns a café in our neighbourhood, a busy happy place where people meet for a coffee, great food and a chat. He has also created a safe space for people who are struggling with life and who need extra support.

His own story is complex. Here's a short version. His mother and aunt were sex workers. He accompanied his mother to the brothel from the age of 11. His father left when he was two years old and his stepfather was abusive. Drug and alcohol abuse led to him attempting suicide some years later, but with the support of professionals and friends he emerged a truly impressive man who feels grateful to have not only survived but thrived.

If I ever feel inclined to have a pity party, I walk down to his café for a coffee with my ageing Border Collie (Barry). I sit in the sun and reflect on how blessed I am while watching Barry try to hump passing dogs with little success and a growled warning from the victim and/or the owner.

Chapter 11

Bits and Pieces

Some of my thoughts on old age don't require a whole chapter, but you may find these interesting or helpful.

Playing the 'Little Old Lady Card'

It pays to use the little old lady card judicially from time to time. I find it particularly helpful in long queues and on public transport. A deep sigh and "oh dear…" in a frail voice, with hand at breast, usually does the trick. Hey, I'm not a saint!

Suffering Fools

I don't suffer fools gladly anymore. I was shopping at our local farmer's market recently with a friend. As we chatted and walked, an older man with a basket of mandarin samples leapt in front of us and said "try my mandarins".

Now I don't particularly like mandarins, so rather than take one of his samples and deplete his stock, I smiled and said "not for me today thanks".

The man wasn't happy and, as I walked away, he shouted after me, "Thanks for NOT supporting Australian farmers!"

I felt angry, but rather than shouting at the man (which I really wanted to do), I calmly walked back to him and started to explain why I hadn't taken one of his samples, and why it wasn't necessary for him to be rude.

He cut me off mid-sentence with a long dialogue about what a difficult week he was having.

Mid-sentence, I put my hand gently on his forearm and said, "I <u>could</u> be dying". Technically, I wasn't lying. We all die eventually.

The man went beet red (I know because he also sold beetroots) and spluttered "are you okay?" Dumb question.

I turned on my heel and left.

Was I wrong in doing this? I don't believe so. I'm weary of people who lash out at strangers because they are unhappy with whatever is going on in their life. They do it without considering the person on whom they are venting and whether they may also be struggling.

And, if I encouraged this man to think about his words before opening his mouth in future, then I have no problem with having stood for myself on that day.

If you don't value yourself, you can't reasonably expect others to do so. You teach people how to treat you.

The Art of Saying "No"

For some women of our generation, it has been hard-wired into our psyche to acquiesce and give until it hurts. But at this stage in our lives, I believe it's our responsibility to live our best lives.

Give yourself time to pause before agreeing to something you really don't want to do. If the person asking can't accept "no" for an answer, particularly if you have reasonably explained why, they aren't considering you or your needs and don't deserve your time.

Take "I should" out of Your Vocabulary

If you hear yourself saying "I should" it probably means you really don't want to. So, don't. However, if you really do think it is important to do something, try saying "I will because…", giving yourself a good reason for whatever it is.

Sage advice from someone who often mutters, "I must lose a little weight" nearly every day as I pour myself another glass of wine, or eat the last piece of chocolate. Don't misunderstand that I take all my own advice!

Postscript

I have loved writing this book. I hope someone reads it, but if not the process has been joyful and satisfying and that's enough. If you have read through to the end, thank you so much.

Thank you, Ben Wier, for the whimsical and wonderful illustrations in my book. They have brought life to my writing and have made me, and I'm sure our readers, laugh with pleasure.

Through typing the text for this book, I have slowly taught myself to use both hands to type again, by retraining my hand and brain. It's still slow, hard work, and at times frustrating, but I make progress every day.

It just goes to show that sometimes change is possible if you want it enough.

Trish Sara.

About the Author

Trish Sara is a 68-year-old grandmother of three, mother of two and wife of 36 years.

She has been a public relations consultant, retailer, website owner and more recently a counsellor specialising in working with mature women.

Throughout her life, she has been a keen observer of others, particularly their relationships and behaviours.

In this, her first book, she makes observations about her own ageing process and offers her conclusions about ageing well, writing anecdotes about these with wisdom, candour and self-deprecating humour.

About the Illustrator

Ben Weir is a Sydney-based illustrator and creative director. Once an aspiring film maker, Ben soon realised he needed to feed his children and switched to his current day job in the glamorous world of advertising.

In between directing events and corporate videos for a diverse set of evil corporations, he finds time to draw. His online comic has been read by at least 6.25 people and he once sold three 'works of art' at a charity auction.

Ben's illustrious career is somewhat charted on his website: www.benweircreative.com.au

www.ingramcontent.com/pod-product-compliance
Lightning Source LLC
Chambersburg PA
CBHW062041290426
44109CB00026B/2691